THRIVE LEADERSHIP

BE SLACKER BETTER

THE KEY TO A MORE SUSTAINABLE AND HEALTHY LEADERSHIP STYLE

STEVE ZONNEVYLLE

Published by Spectrum Education Limited
Lower Hutt, New Zealand
info@spectrumeducation.com

ISBN: 978-1-0670169-1-3

Copyright © Spectrum Education 2024
© Steve Zonnevylle 2024

Designed and typeset by Spectrum Education, New Zealand

This book contains images from
www.canva.com

All rights reserved. No part of this publication may be reproduced, stored in a retrieval system, or transmitted in any form or by any means (electronic, mechanical, photocopying or otherwise), without the prior written permission of both the copyright owner and the publisher of this book.

CONTENTS

INTRODUCTION	01
THE SINGLE USE LIFE	09
YOUR KEY TO BEING SLACKE	15
BE SLACKER AWARE	23
BE SLACKER CLEAR	29
BE FLEXIBLY SLACK	35
BE A SLACK POWERHOUSE	43
BE SLACKER TOGETHER	51
BE A SLACK PROFESSIONAL	59
BE A CREATIVE SLACKER	69
CONCLUSION	77
ABOUT THE AUTHOR	79
THRIVE LEADERS	81

ACKNOWLEDGMENTS

DAVID ARMSTRONG

Thanks David for the many, many hours of discussion, dissection and investigation into this thing that we call leadership. David, your support, advice and all round amazing friendship has helped me many times throughout my career as a Principal. The ideas written in this book owe greatly to the conversations that we have had. Thank you.

KAREN TUI BOYES

Karen, thank you for the time, patience and support that you've given me. You have such a wealth of experiences and amazing ideas that you've shared with me not only throughout the process of writing this book, but also through the Thrive Leadership organisation and Spectrum Education. It's been fantastic to have your support and assistance!

ISABEL GRANADO

Thank you Isabel for all the encouragement, support and love that you have given me during the writing of this book. It's been wonderful to talk through my ideas with you and to gain such a worthwhile and unique perspective from you in terms of management and leadership. Your support has been so heartfelt and inspiring!

ABOUT THE COVER

Daisy is a five year old golden Cocker Spaniel. When this photo was taken, she'd just turned three and she'd just discovered how to hang out the window of the car and soak in all the wonders of the world.

On the face of it, Daisy might appear to be a pretty unusual sort of character to put on the cover of a book about sustainable leadership. I don't know many leadership books that would promote themselves in such a way.

But there's something special about this photo that captures an essence of leadership that is so often overlooked. Daisy is having a wild time. She's loving life to the fullest. All of her senses are working overtime to take in the world around her. She looks like she doesn't have a care in the world. She's living fully in the moment.

Imagine if our leadership style was like this.

This book is about finding ways in your own leadership style in order to enjoy every moment to its fullest - it's here that you'll find ways to thrive.

Be like Daisy - Be Slacker Better.
Steve

One day your life will flash before your eyes. Make sure that it's worth watching.
 - **Gerard Way**

INTRODUCTION

Once upon a time I found myself out on the street in Dunedin. It was a day of shopping, but here I was, in conversation with a long time friend and colleague David Armstrong as I waited for the shopping to conclude. Between us we'd often solve all the problems in the world of education. This day was no different. As I filled in the time between the shops I found myself in a text conversation with Davo.

Between us we'd often solve all the problems in the world of education.

I'm advocating for a change of mindset in the way that you live your professional life

It went something like this:
SZ: There's just so much crap that we have to do day in and day out in our roles that sometimes I forget who I am and why I'm there.
DA: What's the alternative though? Maybe passing all that stuff onto other people?
SZ: Yeah, maybe. Maybe that would free me up to do stuff.
DA: I wonder how you get to delegate it all away and still be a principal, still have the respect of the people you serve without looking slack.
SZ: Maybe we just need to learn to be slacker better ….
DA: LOL

The words sat there for a bit, because initially I didn't really know what I was saying. It was a throw away sort of line.

Then the words began to take on a life of their own as we began to talk about what Being Slacker Better might look like.

I'm always a little surprised at where ideas originate and then how they grow.

In this book I'm going to unpack what Being Slacker Better could look like for you and how it could work in the environment that you work, with the people around you.

My experience is found almost entirely in the education sector, and so I spend most of the time talking from this angle. There's no reason though that an idea like Being Better Slacker couldn't be adapted and used in different contexts.

Initially you might be thinking that I'm advocating for being slack. Likely I'm going to repeat this a lot throughout this book; I'm not suggesting in any way, shape or form that being slack in the conventional sense of the word is the way forward.

Instead I'm advocating for a change of mindset in the way that you live your professional life. This might seem like slacking off to you, considering the way you've gone about things up until now. But over time, you'll learn to see that this is the logical way of letting go of some pretty unsustainable work habits and adopting many better ways of doing and viewing things, making time for you to be you.

A while ago I found myself viewing an old clip online from comedian and TV personality Miranda Hart. Some of you may know her show, "Miranda".

Miranda was talking about life during the covid lockdown and the pressures, stresses and uncertainties that this created for everyone.

She then quoted a guy called Dave Hollis which really took my liking;

"Hear this: in the rush to return to normal, use this time to consider which parts of normal are worth rushing back to."

Bang! Wow! What a great thing to say!

He went on;

"If things go back exactly as they were, we will have missed the opportunity to take the good from this bad. The gift nobody's asked for is sitting here for us all to open — an opportunity to do some housekeeping in where we focus, who we spend time with, what we consume, how we work, what matters and most importantly what doesn't. Take notes. We're getting a lesson we cannot forget when things return to normal."

I liked what this guy Dave was saying. It's true what he was saying in regards to the pandemic and the time that we all spent at home. I wondered if what he said about not wasting the lessons we'd learnt, had indeed been forgotten.

The most important things aren't the things that we do at work but the connections we make.

I wanted to find out more about him. On his Facebook page, he describes himself in this way;

"Every day Dude, In love with Rachel Hollis, Dad x4 Dominating the roads, NYTimes best selling author"

I like this description greatly. I don't even know the guy but in a very small precis he's told me he's not a big noter. He's just an everyday guy who loves his wife and family. Oh, and he's a NY Times best selling author – but that bit comes last.

It resonated with me because it's essentially what I have been promoting for a long time now, that the most important things aren't the things that we do at work but the connections we make.

Given that lockdown is now well and truly in the rearview mirror, I can't help but wonder if we indeed missed a great opportunity to implement something just a little bit revolutionary in terms of how we look at our lives.

We spend so much of our time in our professional lives leading, sorting, being accountable, mentoring, writing screeds of words, connecting, relating and being "fully there".

By the time it's time for our other life, when we leave school each day, there's often little left but to collapse on the couch and nap away the evening in a state of exhaustion.

At present I imagine that our professional Facebook pages would all read like mine;

"Steve Zonnevylle, Educator. Full Stop"

I want to be more like David Hollis' Facebook precis. I want any description of me to start with the most important things.

I want to be proud to be an educator, but I don't want it to define me. I want my role and roles in education to be a part of who I am, but not all of who I am.

For many, using the words 'slacker' and 'educator' in the same sentence is akin to blasphemy! How can we even begin to think of being slack!? How dare we!

So what is the point that I'm trying to make, and how does it relate to Dave Hollis' invitation of not rushing back to normal, given now that we really did ALL rush back to normal, pretty damn fast after the lockdowns?

Being Slacker Better is a call to arms. It's the revolution.

And when better than now? There is never a time better than the present to start things, to think things through, and to begin considering what a new normal might look like. Because, let's face it, the current normal is doing a pretty fantastic job at stressing us all out and making us nothing more than a full stop on a page.

I'm certainly not advocating becoming slack in the conventionally accepted way. Instead, I want you to step up and look at the way you do your job. Take time to look at the habits you've bought into the role over time. I want you to take time to assess the ways that you want to live your life. Big questions indeed.

Take time to look at some of the things that you do now, that you personally would consider slack if you did them differently. Don't worry about the other side of the coin – those things that other people would consider slack if you did them differently. This is your journey, not theirs.

For many, using the words 'slacker' and 'educator' in the same sentence is akin to blasphemy!

For example:

- What if you didn't write so much in your Board Report? (Einstein once said that if you can't explain it simply, then you don't actually understand what you're talking about.)

- What if you worked from home half a day a week?

- What if you left school at 4:00pm on those quieter days?

- What if you closed the door of your office and made yourself unavailable more often?

- What if you spent more time in classrooms and felt confident that administration trivia always has a habit of getting done tomorrow, or the next day?

- What if you viewed your role as being the key relationship maker/connector instead of the key educator?

- What if you didn't have so many meetings?

- What if you looked to maximise your own talents within the school setting more?

- What if you decided not to sweat the small stuff?

- What would happen if …………?

The list goes on, and is limited only by the questions you ask yourself.

In the end, Being Slacker Better is less about some internalised concept of slackness, and more about finding those things that are actually the most important. It's about getting to them more often, because they are the most important things. It's about taking time to work out what is important to you in your life. Not time to do more at school or work, but time to do more in that other time; that time we call "the rest of your life."

This is a very important point. It underlines the premise that being a leader is part of your life, not your whole life.

So to paraphrase Dave Hollis; in the rush to return to normal, let's use this time to consider which parts of normal are worth rushing back to and change those things that are not.

Be Slacker Better!

Being a leader is part of your life, not your whole life

You only live once, but if you do it right, once is enough.
— **Mae West**

CHAPTER ONE
THE SINGLE USE LIFE
IMPACT AND LEGACY

In our lifetime we experience thousands and thousands and thousands of relationships. Some are fleeting like the "how are you doing?" that you said to that old man in the breakfast aisle of the supermarket back in 2013. Others are almost lifelong, like the relationship you might be lucky enough to have with your brother, your sister, or that significant person that was there when you were born, and who will still be there when you pass away.

> In our lifetime we experience thousands and thousands of relationships

Relationships come and go throughout this time, some you remember like they were yesterday and others you forget almost like they never ever happened.

In many ways your life is like a big pond and the relationships are the circulating ripples that rain drops make when they land on the surface. Some drops make very little difference, others cause ripples enough to disrupt the whole pond. Some drops disrupt the pond for your whole life.

It's all of these relationships that make up the flavour of your life; the life that I like to call "A single-use life".

I first thought of this term one day when I was head down in the recycling bin at my house. I was trying to work out which of the plastics were meant to go to the recycling centre and which of them would go to landfill. On the bottom of each plastic bottle, cup, tray, plastic "thing" is a triangle with a number inside it. This tells the human if it can be recycled. The rest of the stuff is classified as single use plastic.

It made me think about my life, and as an extension, everybody's life. We're all living a single-use life.

We're all living a single use life

Yes I guess there could be an argument made that we are recycled too in an ashes to ashes, dust to dust manner. But the life we're living now, in this particular lifetime, isn't recycled. As far as I know we don't get to live this exact life over and over again. That's why I call it a single-use life.

There's something very beautiful about this.

Our single-use life is very unique to us. For the most part we get to choose how we live it and we get to consider the impact and legacy of the life that we lead - if we're lucky.

When our single-use life is over there will be little to be shown for the time that we have used. Our physical impact and legacy on the world will be limited. On average our body will cremate down to 3-5% of our body weight. And that will be about it.

The impact and legacy that we do have is felt most strongly through the relationships we have while we are working with people who (unsurprisingly) are alive now. This is a significant amount of time - for some of us it might equate to 50% of our life. But it's not the total amount of time that we spend in our single-use life.

Once we stop working, and our relationship circles begin to thin, our impact and legacy is felt less.

So what is the legacy and impact that you want to make in your single-use life?

This question reminds me of a story.

A few years ago I found myself sitting in a monthly Board meeting at my school. I was trying to lead a financial discussion down a path that would encourage my fellow board members to release some of our savings. I wanted to see an increase in hours for our Learning Assistants who provided such wonderful support for those children in the school who needed more than what was considered "normal".

The conversation wasn't going quite like I hoped. Some on the board were saying that in order to increase Learning Assistant hours, we'd need to look at the whole operating budget and find some places to cut in order to make ends meet.

I desperately tried to make the point that the operating budget was already stressed, and that we had other money in our savings sitting around doing nothing but gaining interest. I argued that the needs of the current children in the school weren't benefitting from the money sitting in the savings account.

One of the Board members asked a question, "What do you want your legacy to be Steve?"

What is the legacy and impact that you want to make in your single-use life?

Legacy and impact is found in the way that you make people feel

I hadn't ever thought of anything in terms of legacy before.

He went on, "What do you want people to remember you for?"

I struggled to see how this all fits into the finance conversation, but then, as he went on it became clearer.

"Have you ever thought of building a structure that does something that no other building currently does at the school - like a stand alone science lab, or a music room, or a multi-purpose building? We could use our savings for this. Think of your legacy Steve."

I pictured a building with the name ZONNEVYLLE plastered outside, and I wasn't buying it. That's not where I imagined my legacy being.

I've built buildings before, in fact I've built heaps of things in my time as a Principal; playgrounds, tennis courts, swimming pools, multi-purpose use buildings. I've enjoyed a huge sense of achievement and accomplishment building these, but I'm pretty sure that the biggest impact and legacy of my leadership won't be found in these monuments of concrete and mortar.

Earlier this year I found myself driving past one of my old schools. I was there 25 years ago, when I was building stuff. Some of the things I built are still there; some no longer.

About the same time I received a message from a woman who I'd taught at the same school. I'd just moved into a new area, and I'd posted a message on Facebook about needing a dog kennel. The woman had moved a long time ago into my new area. She messaged me: "Mr Zee? Is that you? I loved having you as my teacher when I was an 8 year old, are you still singing the HomeTime Rap?"

The woman made no mention of the buildings that I had built, or of the tennis court that I was so proud of at the time. Instead she was talking about a legacy so much more important - the way that I had made her feel.

Legacy and impact is found predominantly and most powerfully in the relationships that we have with others.

The legacy and impact that you can have on those who you serve isn't related to how many square metres of carpet that you lay but in the way that you make people feel.

Being Slacker Better is part of that legacy and impact building. It's a big part of it.

At the very heart of it you'll find yourself building positive and sustaining relationships. The sort of "human stuff" that makes a real difference in our lives for us all. The stuff that makes people remember how you made them feel and you felt about them.

For the record I didn't win my argument with my Board that night as I tried to put the needs of my students first. Instead, I allowed myself to be sidetracked by a conversation about what my legacy might be. In reality I wonder if we were talking about the "legacy building" of the board member asking the question. This building seemed more like his baby than mine.

Sadly it would take a couple more years before I was able to persuade the Board where the real needs of the school were. This lack of persuasion on my behalf in itself isn't a legacy that I'm particularly proud of; why wasn't I able to make the point clearer to the Board sooner?

The answer is probably found in the fact that at the time, and for much of my time as a Principal, I was pursuing a brand of professionalism called "Please everyone and try to do everything for everyone all the time". It's a common brand found throughout schools in New Zealand. As a result I was a nano-second away at all times from some serious stress burn out. And because of this I simply didn't have the energy to push the big things through that should have been pushed through.

The problem is that we often don't know that we're needing to Be Slacker Better until it's too late.

In your very own single-use life it's all about you. What is your legacy and impact going to be for you?

How will you want you to remember your life?

"Please everyone and try to do everything for everyone all the time" Professionalism

The meaning of life is that it is to be lived.
— **Bruce Lee**

CHAPTER TWO
YOUR KEY TO BEING SLACKER
VISION AND MEANING

Let's get started into crafting your personal vision and finding meaning as a leader with the purpose of Being Slacker Better.

Think of it this way; If you were a captain of your own ship, charting a course through the vast sea of life, (of which leadership is a part), it would be really useful to know exactly where you were going. Before you set sail you need something useful to guide you through the choppy waters. That's where your personal vision and meaning comes in.

> Being Slacker Better is about giving you permission to live the life you want to live

At the very heart of it, Being Slacker Better is about giving yourself the permission to live the life that you want to live. The problem is that many of us don't know what that life really looks like. We can't see it because we don't have a vision of what it might look like. Most of the time we're simply too busy to take the time to even think about it.

To be honest, I used to find myself feeling really anxious when people asked me about my vision. All I could think about is what they would think. Then I'd stress even more when I heard them share their version. Their vision was always better than mine!

I'd get bogged down in some sort of never ending judgement loop. To me it seemed better not to have a vision at all.

I spent far too long in this mindset; years even.

Truth is your particular vision doesn't have to be some mystical prophecy or grandiose statement carved in stone. No, it's more like a vivid painting of the future you want to create.
Close your eyes and imagine your ideal world. The emphasis here is on the word YOUR. Get that clear in your head. This isn't someone else's ideal world - it's yours.

What does it look like? How does your family fit into this picture? If you're a leader how does your team fit into this picture? How do you fit into this picture?

Make your vision clear enough to inspire you first, before inspiring those people who you lead. Make it flexible enough to weather any storm that comes your way, because as you know, storms come and go - they always have and always will.

This flexibility is the slackness in your vision that you need.

For me, mine is very direct. I don't really care if it sounds wishy washy, hippy sounding, or just plain airy fairy to other people. None of that matters. The only thing that matters is that it sounds like me and conveys what I want to do in my life.

This is mine:

> "In my life I want to love who I'm with; love who I am; love what I'm doing and love where I am going."

Meaning is the stuff that not only gets you out of bed each day, it keeps you out of bed.

Even now I feel slightly anxious about writing this down and sharing it. But really, who cares. What difference does it make if someone doesn't like it; or even if someone else loves it. At the end of the day your vision is all about you and no one else.

Now, let's find some meaning. I'm a big fan of this word. I like it way better than purpose, even though they can mean similar things. I guess I consider "meaning" and "purpose" as being two rowers in a boat, but with slightly different strengths.

Meaning to be me is all the stuff that adds depth and richness to your life. It's that sense of fulfilment and satisfaction you get from the things you do— it's the joy of making a difference, the satisfaction of a job well done, or the warmth of connecting with others. It's about finding significance and value in the everyday moments, whether big or small. It's your reason for being here on planet Earth.

This is really important stuff. Meaning is the stuff that not only gets you out of bed each day, it keeps you out of bed.
Purpose on the other hand is more like the set of instructions that gives your life direction and focus. It's definitely important as it's the guiding star that keeps you on course when the seas get rough. But without meaning, the purpose becomes all a little mute.

I found in my role as a school Principal for nearly 30 years that there was always plenty of purpose in what I did. There's no doubt that this gave me direction, but often it came with little meaning; or even worse kept me distracted from finding any true meaning. I got lost in the mountains of papers that I shuffled around on my desktop. As a result, I lost my way far too many times that I'd care to admit.

Meaning isn't only about looking into some distant time, it's also about finding fulfilment and satisfaction in the present moment. This is the oil that keeps those gears moving. Without meaning you might as well just be a shadow. If you can find meaning in your purpose then you're really onto something. But purpose without meaning is just a damp squib. When you have purpose without meaning you open yourself up to "just working for the man". And that becomes pretty demoralising damn quickly.

Being Slacker Better is about finding that meaning in your day to day life. The "slacker" part is about making time and finding space, often away from the mundane purpose of the day, to find the meaning in what you're doing.

I'm a big fan of Viktor Frankl. Frankl spent a long time in Nazi Concentration Camps during World War Two. He was subjected to many, many awful things, and asked to do some incredibly dehumanising tasks. The tasks all had some sort of purpose, many with evil intent, but they were bereft of meaning. He found solace, and ultimately survival, in discovering meaning in everything and anything around him. He found meaning in the strangest and most unusual places. This by no-means meant that he supported and appreciated what he was doing. Quite the opposite, as he suffered greatly for years, and saw terrible inhuman things daily. But it was the process of finding some sort of meaning that eventually kept him alive.

"Between stimulus and response, there is a space. In that space is our power to choose our response. In our response lies our growth and our freedom."
- Viktor Frankl.

Being Slacker Better is about finding that space. We naturally feel uneasy, and even lazy (or slack) because we think we're wasting time and being taken away from the purpose at hand when we are in this space. In reality we're doing important work. Finding that meaning is key.

Meaning is the fuel that keeps you running not only during the good times, but also when the going gets tough. It's the 'Why do you do what you do?'; the " What gets you out of bed in the morning (besides the promise of coffee)?".

Maybe you're passionate about empowering others, driving change, or building something awesome from the ground up. Maybe you love the thrill of creating stuff, or working alongside someone to support them in their own meaning - whatever it is, that's not slack at all, let it light a fire in your belly and guide your every move.

"Between stimulus and response, there is a space. In that space is our power to choose our response. In our response lies our growth and our freedom."
- Viktor Frankl.

Play around with different words and phrases until you find the perfect fit.

Ok, so now that we've got the basics down, it's time to get specific.

Let's talk about values.

These are like the guiding principles that steer your ship. A quick google search tells us that there are over 200 words in the English language that convey value like meaning.

To be honest, we could spend all day writing lists of values, arguing about their own specific meaning, and then aligning them to ourselves. Instead I recommend the VIA.

The VIA (Values in Action) Institute on Character is a non-profit organisation that focuses on promoting the science of character strengths and virtues. It was founded by Dr. Martin Seligman and Dr. Christopher Peterson, both eminent psychologists, as part of the broader positive psychology movement.

If you go to the website https://www.viacharacter.org you can undertake a free assessment that will tell you what your five core value strengths are.

I recommend taking this assessment and once you know your top five hold onto them tightly. And although they'll certainly be your compass when you're navigating tricky waters, they're even more likely to help you find meaning in whatever you get up to during the ordinary "normal" times of your life.

Ok, so what about your team? How do you want them to feel when they're working with you? Inspired? Supported? Like they're part of something bigger than themselves? Your vision and meaning should speak to them too. From this you'll be better able to define a sense of purpose when working with you.

Now, here's the fun part: putting it all together. Grab a pen and paper and start jotting down ideas.

I like the physicality of writing things down with a big black vivid pen and a huge piece of paper. There's nothing like having a clear, white, A3 pad sitting in front of you waiting to be written and scribbled all over.

Play around with different words and phrases until you find the perfect fit. Don't worry about making it sound fancy or polished—this is just for you. Take your time.

Vision

Friends

Family

time to be me!

Being creative in my job

having time to invest in others

LOVE

enjoying stuff

Once you've got something that feels right, go ahead and share it if you want. But in reality it's no biggie if you don't, not at this stage anyway. This is something very personal to you.

It's your statement of intent, no one else's.

It's your key to being slack.

beauty

being authentic in everything I do

finding meaning in the day to day things in my life and living my life that way

working out what being professional really means to me

There is an old-fashioned word for the body of skills that emotional intelligence represents: character.
– **Daniel Goleman**

CHAPTER THREE
BE SLACKER AWARE
EMOTIONAL INTELLIGENCE

Our leadership roles are often so crazy and diverse, as we experience the rollercoaster of any given day, that we seldom stop to wonder exactly why.

Chances are it's all emotionally fueled. Therefore being emotionally intelligent is crucial.

Let's spend a little time talking about how emotional intelligence can help us Be Slacker Better, and how Being Slacker Better can help us be more emotionally aware.

Being Slacker Better can help us be more emotionally aware

First things first, let's talk about self-awareness. This should be your number one superpower. Chances are that if you find yourself constantly getting stressed, lashing out at people, blowing a fuse, and losing the plot then self-awareness isn't one of your super powers.

Self awareness is that thing that lets you tune into your own emotions and understand how they're affecting your thoughts and actions and any given moment in time.

Think of it a bit like an emotional radar that helps you navigate the ups and downs of leadership (and life as a whole) without crashing and burning.

Self-awareness is the key to understanding those times when you need to give yourself some slack.

Being self-aware isn't hard though - but it does take some practice.

So, take a moment to check in with yourself. How are you feeling emotionally right now? What's driving those feelings? How are you feeling physically right now? Is your heart racing? What sort of thoughts are flying through your head? Are they nice thoughts? Do they make you feel yuck?

Consider how you feel when "such and such" happens - you know when you hear the phone ring and your secretary tells you it's Mrs Jones from across the road on the line; or when your standing in front of a large auditorium of 800 people; or when little Jimmy has kicked in a brand new TV screen; or when your Deputy Principal has done something completely against your instructions - what sort of feelings do you get? How do you react instantly?

In these times self awareness is key.

I used to practise self awareness regularly throughout the day. I'd actually set the alarm on my phone to go off four times a day just to remind myself to have a check in. Sometimes I'd write these experiences down in journal form. Pretty quickly I began to get a picture as to how I was experiencing the roller coaster of my professional life.

Self-awareness is the key to understanding those times when you need to give yourself some slack.

Empathy is about stepping into someone else's shoes and seeing the world through their eyes.

As I got better at this I began noticing that I'd naturally give myself a quick 'check in' during other random times during the day. Especially so, just prior to "losing it". The first time I did this was very telling. A student had just jumped the fence and ran off down the road shouting abuse at whoever chased him, threatening to throw rocks at the passing cars. I had a quick 'check in' with myself and found that I was getting pretty angry - nothing surprising about that! This kid was just about to interrupt and stuff up the rest of my well planned day, spreading this kind of chaos throughout the neighbourhood. Getting angry wasn't the answer in this situation. And yes, my day was interrupted, and more than stuffed up, but being angry was never going to bring that back. This needed a calm head. And that's what the situation got - a calm head.

Back to Viktor Frankl's quote, "Between stimulus and response, there is a space. In that space is our power to choose our response. In our response lies our growth and our freedom."

That space is where your Self Awareness can sit really nicely; that space is your time to take stock of what is happening and to think about what is the BEST thing to happen next; that space is where you give yourself some slack.

Once you've got a handle on your own emotions, you can start leading with intention and authenticity.

Authenticity is another one of those words that I've never really been a big fan of. It seemed to pop up out of nowhere in the mid 2010's and has been with us ever since. To be honest, I just prefer 'being real'.

Being Self Aware helps you to be real in real life situations. This means taking on situations as you, at your best and as you find them, not as someone else wants you to find them. It's about giving it all a good solid dosing of this magical thing called you.

Now let's talk about empathy.

Empathy is one of those things that fits snuggly in the Be Slacker Better kete and is crucial to enhancing your emotional intelligence.

Empathy is about stepping into someone else's shoes and seeing the world through their eyes. The next time a team member comes to you with a problem, take time to really listen. There is a lot to be learnt by tuning into their emotions, validating their feelings, and showing them that you care. This all goes a long way when it comes to building trust and rapport not only as a leader, but also as a great human being.

Being Self Aware allows you to show greater empathy to those around you. Empathy takes time though and in tricky and challenging situations there may be other people around you who question whether being empathetic is the best way forward.

There were many times in my career when I was accused of being far too soft in situations; or far too lenient; or plainly just far too slack in the manner in which I approached a difficult situation. I felt those accusations and judgments acutely and at times I struggled to keep it "real" in the manner that met with my own values. There were sleepless nights as a result.

But being empathetic is key to understanding how the people around you work. One of the roles that you have as a leader is to get the best out of the people that you support. This means having a solid understanding of who they are, what makes them tick, and what makes them, them.

Being Slacker Better is about giving not only yourself some slack, but also those around you. I'd always argue that playing the long game, by being empathetic, self aware and understanding, will pay much bigger dividends then short, sharp, shift sorts of retaliatory strategies.

This means giving yourself some slack though when it comes to the disappointments that will still no doubt come your way. This isn't always easy to do - especially so at 3am in the morning.

But being self aware of how you're feeling about something can certainly help you cope. Give yourself some slack during these times; afterall you're only human.

Last but not least, let's talk about relationship management.

Relationship management requires oodles and oodles of emotional intelligence.

This is like the glue that holds your team together. It's about building strong, supportive relationships with not only your team members, but also everyone that you serve as a leader. Fostering a culture of trust, respect, and open communication is just so vital to any situation that requires leadership from you.

Relationship management requires great emotional dexterity, flexibility and all round skill. There will be times when you're bound to get it all hopelessly wrong.

Relationship management requires oodles and oodles of emotional intelligence

Having an attitude of Being Slacker Better can help greatly during these times. It's about embracing this little thing called "being a human" and celebrating the fact that you can never get a consistently perfect 10/10 score in anything that involves a human relationship.

Remember, it's not about being perfect or having all the answers. It's about showing up, tuning in, and leading with heart. So go ahead, embrace your emotions, lead with empathy, be self aware but take time to give yourself some slack during those times when things don't go quite to plan.

Leading from the heart

The single biggest problem in communication is the illusion that it has taken place.
- **George Bernard Shaw**

CHAPTER FOUR
BE SLACKER CLEAR
COMMUNICATING WITH INTENT

When we first started talking about Being Slacker Better it seemed to cause great consternation; controversy even.

At one conference we hoped to call our presentation "Be Slacker Better", but it was deemed by the organisers as promoting something just a little bit negative. As a result we had to name the talk something else. I've got no idea what the title was - obviously it wasn't particularly memorable!

> There's nothing new in saying that it's important for leaders to give themselves a break

To be honest Being Slacker Better isn't a new thing at all. There's nothing new in saying that it's important for leaders to give themselves a bit of a break from time to time, especially in these times of world wide stress and uncertainty. All I've done is give it a provocative name.

However online I've battled with teachers who have told me that I'm advocating laziness; that I'm all about accepting something mediocre; and that excellence in my world has literally flown the coop. None of this is true.

As a result I've spent quite a lot of time talking about the differences between "Being Slacker Better" and "Being a Better Slacker". To me they're in different universes in terms of meaning.

Being Slacker Better is about allowing yourself some slack during those times that are particularly challenging, and in those important times just afterwards, so that you can appropriately recover in the true sense of the term well-being. And then, after you've recovered you can be in a much better spot to be truly excellent and totally beyond mediocre.

Being a Better Slacker on the other hand is about finding the couch, a great movie on Netflix, a beer in one hand and a stash of chocolate in the other, and spending all day there - moving only to refill the beer or to get more chocolate.

There is a time when both are just fine. Definitely, maybe.

Let's just stick with Being Slacker Better

Being Slacker Better is about getting the best out of yourself and your team and it doesn't involve putting on weight! It's about giving yourself a much-needed mental break and reassessing how you perceive your performance in your professional life based on both your well-being and what you want out of your life. That last part is crucial; what do you want out of your life?

How we communicate this to others is important. We really don't want people to think that your very own interpretation of being professional revolves around a notion of laziness and slackness.

Communication has always been that magical ingredient that can make or break this message in your leadership game. As a leader you're the conductor of a wonderful symphony orchestra, and your words are the notes that bring the music to life. Whether you're leading a team meeting, giving feedback, or just informally talking with your colleagues over a coffee, quality communication is key to keeping everyone in tune and on beat. This is the same for any idea that you want to introduce to the people you serve.

What's slack about that?

How you convey this message of Being Slacker Better is key.

So let's talk about clarity. With all the messages that you give your team, clarity is vital. I've already talked about how people can get the message wrong, or interpret what you're saying when you use the word, slack. It can go pear shaped if you haven't gotten your own thinking nice and clear.

It's therefore vital that you take time to unpack exactly what you mean before you start talking to others in your team. Keep it simple though; keep it clear; and be concise.

Start with the vision that you wrote in Chapter 2. Once you know what you're actually about and you've committed to that vision, you can begin to let people know what's written on that rock that you stand on.

There's always a vulnerability in this conversation. You might feel a bit uncomfortable at first. But stick with your vision, and keep committed to your message.

For me, my vision is my message: In my life I want to love what I'm doing; love who I'm with; love who I am; and love where I am going.

I like to get a bit provocative here and so I ask the question; "What's slack about that?"

Talk with them about your values and where you find meaning in your professional role.

I'd do this by sharing my VIA values strengths (check out Chapter 2). I'd paint a word picture that shows how my top five value strengths give me meaning in my job and as a result enhance the vision I have for my life. This in turn greatly improves my daily chances of meeting that vision and being well.

Again I ask the question; "What's slack about that?"

Being Slacker Better is about giving yourself the permission to make room in your busy professional life to align yourself to the vision you have for your life; your whole life. There's nothing particularly slack about that either, especially when you're considering that your life is a very long time and that it'll go on, way beyond your working life.

However in a school, business or work place, having a Be Slacker Better attitude is giving everyone that permission, it's not all about you. It's a game for the whole family! It's not really about being slack at all; it's more about taking a look at what is culturally considered in your place as being professional - having a robust conversation about that - and then doing something about that!

Now it's time to be a listener. Leaders need to be great listeners. I always love to use the saying that goes, "We have two ears and one mouth for a reason". As a leader you should really abide by this!

The acronym, WAIT is also pretty clever; Why Am I Talking? Give enough space to the conversation so that everyone can say their bit. Silence can be uncomfortable, and I'm always filling it with something stupid to say, so don't be a Steve and instead give your team that room.

It's important to tune into what others are saying; really hear them out, show them that you care about what they have to say. Start by talking with them about their own vision for their life.

You can help by asking the following questions:

- Does your vision for your life fit in with your whole life or do you separate your work life from the rest of your life?

- What does being a professional really mean to you?

- Currently is there a gap between your vision for your life and what you consider to be professional in your work life? If there is, why is that so?

- Are there times in your work life that you feel slack because you've put your own well-being needs first?

- How has this made you feel?

- Questions like this help your team be self aware.

And here you can ask again; "What's slack about that?"

Why **A**m **I T**alking?

Giving slack is often necessary for manoeuvring a boat

In Chapter Three I talked about the importance of having the emotional intelligence quality of empathy.

Good communication isn't just about words—it's about emotions too. It's important here that you are able to share an empathy for what your team is sharing with you. There will undoubtedly be things in the conversation that you lead that may be a little confronting, and emotional. Be aware of this and show empathy when and if needed.

There may even still be conversations about how it seems "impossible" to be both slack and professional at the same time. Maybe some people will still bristle at this term, slack.

It may be useful to remind people of what slackness means in a nautical sense. You see, giving something slack on the ocean waves means allowing some looseness or freedom in a line or rope. This could involve easing the tension on a line to allow a boat to drift or move more freely, or letting out additional rope to accommodate movement or changes in the position of the vessel.

Giving slack is often necessary for manoeuvring a boat safely, especially when adjusting sails, docking, or dealing with changing wind or tide conditions.

Giving slack also means that you can tighten up in other areas, also to deal with changing winds or conditions.

This is a useful metaphor to help people start thinking about bridging any professional vs slack divide. And from this position you can then start looking at how Being Slacker Better could improve your workplace.

No matter what twists and turns your life offers you, your ability to be adaptable and flexible will help you to stay open to all of the hidden gifts that difficulty may offer.
– **Mandy Ingber**

CHAPTER FOUR
BE FLEXIBLY SLACK
ADAPTABILITY AND RESILIENCE

Keeping slightly with the nautical metaphor when I was a kid I spent my fair share of time in bathtubs playing with rubber ducks.

There's two things I learnt about this play.
1. If you have multiple Rubber Ducks it's always difficult to get them all in a row, especially when the bath water is choppy.
2. When the water gets rough and the bubbles start swirling, what do the rubber ducks do? They roll with the waves, bobbing and bouncing back like they own the bath. They never sink.

It's hard to keep all your ducks in a row

That's adaptability and resilience in action. As a leader, one of your most important roles is to navigate any challenging times as though you're a rubber duck in choppy bathwater.

Once again, there may be people who bristle at this so-called 'unprofessional' analogy and being labelled as 'rubber ducks'. First, I talk about being slack, and now I'm talking about rubber ducks? What's next!?

I'm going to give myself some slack here, and I'm going to let this sort of judgement flow off me like - well, like water off a rubber ducky's back!

So let's first talk about adaptability.

Adaptability is a bit like the air in the rubber duck that keeps you buoyant. It helps you roll with the punches and pivot like a ballerina when life throws you a curveball and keeps you afloat.

Adaptability is like the air in a rubber duck that keeps you buoyant.

Our lives, both personal and professional, are always prone to sudden changes in plans, to new projects landing on your desk, or to even a global pandemic turning the world upside down. Adaptability is about embracing the chaos and finding creative solutions on the fly all without batting an eye.

When talking out loud about Being Slacker Better it can be akin to a sudden change of plan. It can be unsettling at first.

The best teams will be just like rubber ducks and they'll be adaptable. So too should you.

You might have great plans for Being Slacker Better to transform your school or workplace overnight. However like all great ideas, it will take time to stick and the real work comes in working on the culture of your place. You do this by starting with the communication process I talked about in the previous chapter.

The beauty of Being Slacker Better of course is that it is so adaptable. It's something that is unique to each person. It's a personal mindset more than an actual piece of work. But any work that involves culture change, as Being Slacker Better potentially is, may take time, and so be prepared to be adaptable.

It's quite likely that one or more of the following will pop up to disrupt your plans:

- Life intervening - anything can happen and it most probably will

- Running out of steam - change takes energy

- New people joining your team - people come and go all the time

- Running out of time - time is finite

Be adaptable, and rubber duck like by:

- Being realistic - things happen all the time. It's very rare indeed to get all your ducks in a row. Do what you can.

- Understanding your people - people have finite energy reserves. Keep an eye on them, assess the climate of your team to see if people have had enough, for the time being. There's always tomorrow, or next week, or next term.

- Talking and listening - keep your ears to the ground, and adapt your plans as you see fit according to what you hear. Maybe you can move things along faster, but speed, or maybe even lack of it is always key!

- Positive retention - chances are that if you have happy people on your team that you'll find that the "keeping people on your team" part will look after itself. However sometimes people do come and go. Consider in your interview process asking questions about the individual's vision for themselves. Do they align with your school's culture?

- Timetabling - look at the timetable of the year or term and work out the stress points. Avoid big stuff during these stress points.

Now, let's talk about resilience. This is like the superpower that helps you bounce back from setbacks and may be even stronger than ever. In a rubber duck sense, resilience is about bobbing along on the surface of the waves even when you've been dunked a few times. It's all about dusting yourself off, picking yourself up, and powering through adversity, sometimes even with a smile on your face.

Assess the climate of your team to see if they've had enough.

Being Slacker Better is all about building resilience.

Let me take you back a little. It's June 2022. In New Zealand, the autumn has turned to winter and the frigid weather outside is doing everything it can to make itself inside. At the same time we're all coping with a worldwide pandemic and we're all furiously pulling out every adaptable trick in the book.

Around us people are using the word resilient a lot. So much so that the word itself is travelling at pandemic speed. At first the word catches on like a call to arms. It's on the tip of everyone's tongue - we can all get through this because we are resilient.

But over time, as the pandemic and its lockdown effects continue, it feels that even being resilient won't be enough.

I'm sitting in a meeting. As I said, the weather is trying desperately to come inside. In front of us stands someone from the Ministry of Education. She is doing everything she can to keep the conversation in the room from turning cold like the weather outside.

Being Slacker Better is all about building resilience.

Years later I think she probably did the very best that she could - maybe even better. But at the time her assurances to the room full of school principals that all would be fine left us all colder. Then she pulled out the word resilient. All we needed to do was to be just a little bit more resilient, she told us. I just about choked on the ice cold air.

You see, we use these words, like resilient, like they're the elixir of life; that they'll solve everything. But we're never really told what they actually mean or how they're going to make any difference.

On reflection I wonder if she'd have been better to tell us all to "Be Slacker Better". That would have meant a lot more to me. It would've told me that it was ok to let go, just a little bit, and to take time (just a little bit) to look after my own well-being. And that, this, in turn, would give me the resilience to move forward.

Resilience isn't just something that comes along and that can be automatically applied. It's not like a bandaid on a bleeding wound. It takes time and Being Slacker Better is a perfect way of building resilience for you and the people that you serve.

Here are some ideas that help build resilience:

- **Set the Tone:** Start by creating a culture where resilience is celebrated. Talk openly about setbacks and failures, and highlight the lessons learned from them. Being Slacker Better lets your team know that it's okay to stumble, and it's fine to pick themselves back up and keep moving forward when they do. People around them will "pick up the slack" while they're getting it together, because that's what great teams do.

- **Lead by Example:** Show your team what resilience looks like in action. Promote a sense of Being Slacker Better. When faced with challenges, stay calm, stay positive, and tackle problems head-on. Let your team see that you're not afraid to roll up your sleeves and get your hands dirty, but also that you're not afraid to show that you are human and fallible. Maybe you also need a break from time to time.

- **Foster Support:** Encourage your team to lean on each other for support. Create opportunities for collaboration and teamwork, and emphasise the importance of looking out for one another. A strong support network can make all the difference when times get tough. Being Slacker Better means asking for help when you need it. You don't need to be overly proud and that you can " cope on your own" when really a little bit of help can go a long way.

- **Celebrate Progress:** Acknowledge and celebrate small wins along the way. Whether it's overcoming a minor setback or reaching a milestone, take the time to recognise and appreciate your team's efforts. Positive reinforcement can help boost morale and keep spirits high. If there is a time not to be slack - do it during times of celebration! Go over the top!

- **Encourage Self-Care:** Remind your team to take care of themselves, both mentally and physically. This is key Be Slacker Better stuff. Encourage breaks, offer flexible work arrangements when possible, and provide resources for managing stress and maintaining work-life balance. A healthy, happy team is a resilient team.

- **Provide Learning Opportunities:** Encourage your team to embrace challenges as opportunities for growth. Offer training, mentorship, and development opportunities to help them build new skills and increase their confidence in their ability to overcome obstacles. Be open about talking about personal goals - allow your team to openly question the meaning they get from their work.

- **Stay Flexible:** This is very Be Slacker Better like. Be prepared to adapt and adjust your plans as needed. Resilience isn't about stubbornly sticking to a course of action no matter what—it's about being flexible and resourceful in the face of change. So, be willing to pivot when necessary and keep your eyes on the horizon.

If you think about it, building adaptability and resilience isn't just about weathering the storm yourself. It's about creating a culture where your team feels supported, empowered, and encouraged to grow, so that you can all weather the storms. By all means, lead by example, but also let your team take the lead.

Show your team that it's okay to make mistakes, it's okay to fail, and it's okay to ask for help when you need it. Be their biggest cheerleader, their strongest supporter, and their shoulder to lean on when times get tough. But also find ways to get the support you need. You might feel a little slack asking for help, but when you build a team of rubber ducks who aren't afraid to roll with the waves, there's no challenge you won't overcome.

There are two ways to spread the light – to be the candle, or to be the mirror that reflects it – **Edith Wharton**

CHAPTER FIVE
BE A SLACK POWERHOUSE
EMPOWERMENT AND DELEGATION

There's no doubt that being a leader can be a profoundly lonely and isolating position to be in.

Sometimes it just plainly sucks.

Around you people are expecting great things of you.

Inside your head you're expecting great things from you.

You don't want to fail.

You don't want to let anyone down.

> Around you, people are expecting great things of you

This is true throughout your career as a leader, but it's even harder to get your head around when you're just beginning.

In your mind you're telling yourself that you don't want to come across as being slack. You get paid the big bucks after-all.

Truth is, this is just a perception that you're buying into. It might be the current reality, but that's basically because you've done all you can to make it so. Truth is you never really are being slack, or are ever going to be slack.

As a result you've found yourself arriving at work early; being one of the last to leave at night; eating your lunch at your desk; and saying "Hell yes!" to everything and everyone that moves.

Initially everyone has loved you for it!

This works just fine for a while.

Well, until it doesn't.

After a while people begin to wonder where they fit into things

After a while the people around you begin to wonder where they fit into the big scheme of things. And they begin to get pretty annoyed when you start to drop the many balls that you're currently juggling.

Ironically they begin to think that you're slack because you keep on dropping the ball. They don't see what's going on in your head; they're not lying beside you at 3am when you're wide awake. They don't climb inside your skull and see the mish mash of ideas, worries and stresses that clammer to be addressed.

Instead they just see you struggling and they come to their own conclusions as to why this is so. Inevitably they taint this impression with the own struggles that they're going through.

Ok, sure, I'm not talking about everyone. There will be some on your team who appreciate what you're doing. But it's likely that everyone around you is also going through their own crap, and so it's natural for them to just think of you in simpler terms; you're doing good or you're doing bad.

People talk. And they like to share their impressions of you as a leader with others. You know this, and so the pressure not to be slack, to do a damn good job, just multiplies itself.

Now where's the fun in all that? Where has your vision for what you want in your life gone?

The best leaders in the world get around all this by learning quickly how to delegate. But the best of them don't do this just by saying "do this, and do that". Instead they find ways to empower their team.

Empowering your team for you as leader starts with stepping out of the limelight. Initially this seems counterintuitive to what you may have learnt growing up about what leadership is all about. But it's a crucial point.

To build a great team you need to provide the people around you with lots of opportunity to step up and step into the limelight. It's a little bit like sharing the superhero cape that you were given when you took on the role as their leader.

Handing out superhero capes to your team and giving them the power to save the day has many, many advantages. These include:

Motivation: Knowing they have the power to "save the day" can be incredibly motivating for your team members. It gives everyone a sense of purpose and drive to excel in their work.

Team Spirit: When everyone feels like a superhero, it fosters a strong sense of camaraderie and teamwork. Suddenly they're not just individual contributors; they're part of a unified force working towards a common goal.

Creativity: Superheroes often have to think outside the box to overcome challenges. Giving your team members the "power" to be superheroes encourages creative problem-solving and innovation.

Resilience: Superheroes face setbacks and obstacles but always find a way to overcome them. By encouraging your team to embrace their inner superhero, you're promoting resilience and the ability to bounce back from failures.

- **Leadership Development:** When team members feel empowered, they're more likely to take initiative and demonstrate leadership qualities. This can lead to the development of future leaders within your organisation.

- **Positive Culture:** Embracing a superhero mentality can contribute to a positive and uplifting organisational culture. It fosters a sense of fun, excitement, and positivity in the workplace. Maybe it's time to have a superhero dress up day in the office!

- **Satisfaction:** Just like superheroes save the day for those in need, empowered and motivated team members are more likely to go above and beyond to satisfy others and to be satisfied themselves. They'll pick up the slack without question when called upon.

- **Adaptability:** Superheroes often face unexpected challenges and must adapt quickly to changing circumstances. Encouraging your team to see themselves as superheroes can promote adaptability and agility in the face of change.

- **Personal Growth:** Finally, embracing their inner superhero can lead to personal growth and development for individual team members. They may discover new strengths and abilities they didn't know they had.

The advantage to you, (both as a leader and as a human being), in building an empowering culture in your workplace is that it allows you to Be Slacker Better. In fact it does it almost by magic; by stealth. Not only that, it allows **EVERYONE** to Be Slacker Better. All of this makes you a fantastic leader.

When you're empowering others in your team, you're getting much needed slack in the rope to work at a higher level. It frees you up to be more aware, not only of the place that you work in, but also of your own personal state of being.

You get to move back to your vision - your vision of being - and you get to work on this to make it a day by day reality.

Your old self would call this being slack, because you'd feel that you were no longer keeping a tight, tight grip on the day to day business of your workplace. The reality is that you *are* working on the business.

If you are in a position where you are consistently and sustainably "well" then, just like you, your business will thrive.

Empowering people isn't always as easy as it sounds. Communication is crucial and it's important that everyone has a firm understanding of "what's in it for them".

When I was a Principal I was always worried that passing on work to my teachers would do two things:

1. It would over work them and take them away from their core roles
2. It would make them feel resentful towards me - like I wasn't doing anything at all

Both of these things aren't good.

So it's back to open and clear two-way communication, and just as importantly, knowing your team and all their individual strengths really well.

When it comes to communication, being clear on why you're letting the reins go a little is crucial.

When it comes to communication, being clear on why you're letting the reins go a little is crucial.

How do you go about empowering people then? Here are some ideas, but I'd like to preface this list by saying that I didn't always succeed.

Working with people is always an "on-going" sort of gig; you never really are ever finished! There will always be someone on your team who doesn't quite buy into your vision, or (let's face it), even like you.

There were times when I was accused of favouritism, or cronyism and probably a whole lot of other "'isms".

Sometimes it's near impossible to please everyone, but if you can get the culture right then you can come close.

- **Delegate Authority:** Trust your team members to take on responsibilities and make decisions within their areas of expertise. Delegate tasks and projects that allow them to showcase their skills and grow professionally. Let them shine!

- **Provide Autonomy:** Give your team members the freedom to work independently and make decisions without micromanagement. Micromanagement is an empowerment killer! Encourage them to take ownership of their work and find their own solutions to challenges.

- **Set Clear Expectations:** Clearly communicate your expectations regarding goals, objectives, and performance standards. Ensure that your team understands what is expected of them and how their work contributes to the overall success of the team and organisation. Give them a timeline and time to get it all done.

- **Provide Feedback:** Offer regular feedback, both positive and constructive, to help your team members grow and improve. Acknowledge their achievements and provide guidance on areas where they can develop their skills further.

- **Encourage Learning and Development:** Support your team members' professional growth by providing opportunities for training, learning, and skill development. Encourage them to pursue new challenges and expand their knowledge and expertise.

- **Promote Collaboration:** Foster a collaborative work environment where team members feel comfortable sharing ideas, collaborating on projects, and learning from one another. Encourage open communication and create opportunities for teamwork and cross-functional collaboration. Being Slacker Better is finding efficient ways to be collaborative. It doesn't have to be "all on one person"; share the load.

- **Recognise and Reward Achievements:** Acknowledge and celebrate the achievements and successes of your team members. Recognise their hard work, dedication, and contributions to the team's goals. Offer rewards, incentives, or other forms of recognition to show your appreciation. I'm not talking about monetary rewards either - sometimes the best rewards come from the heart.

- **Lead by Example:** Lead by example and demonstrate the behaviours and attitudes you want to see in your team members. Show integrity, professionalism, and a commitment to excellence in your own work, and your team is likely to follow suit.

- **Create a Positive Work Environment:** Foster a positive and inclusive work environment where team members feel valued, respected, and supported.

- **Encourage diversity of thought** and perspective and promote a culture of collaboration, trust, and mutual respect.

The best rewards always come from the heart

If you get things just right, then everyone gets to Be Slacker Better. You'll find that a natural understanding begins to permeate through your school or work place.

That understanding looks a little like this:

We all have 24 hours a day to live our lives. If we're lucky a good proportion of this, (maybe up to a third), is spent asleep. The rest is split between work and all the stuff outside work. This split changes all the time and is what we like to call "the work/life balance". However much time we spend in these two places is immaterial. What's more important is the quality of that time that we experience.

Being Slacker Better is about actively pursuing and promoting that quality of time. It's that quality of time where you find the meaning in your life.

Empowering your team helps you do just that.

Together we can.
– **Anonymous**

CHAPTER SIX
BE SLACKER TOGETHER
COLLECTIVE WELL BEING

Ok, so far we've talked about building your own vision, supporting your emotional intelligence, communicating in a way that both clarifies and demystifies, being adaptable and resilient and empowering the people around you.

Essentially we've said;

- Be clear in your mind personally about what drives you in your life
- Be aware of how you tick emotionally
- Be open to others
- Be adaptable
- And let go of the reins

If you've got this all sorted then you're well on the way to Being Slacker Better. In fact you're getting to the Being Slacker **FOR THE** Better stage.

That's impressive!

Next I want to spend some time talking about Being Slacker Together and encouraging Collective well-being.

These are very much linked to the last chapter when I talked about empowerment.

The difference is that Collective well-being is where Being Slacker Better becomes sustainable.

You don't want this new way of thinking and doing things, to be some flash in the pan. You want it embedded in the very fabric of how you see things, plan things and do things in your school or work place.

It's all very well to give a whole heap of people on your team superhero capes and then tell them to go off and "Be Slacker Better". With that there will always be a lack of purpose and then everyone really will become slack in the negative and bad meaning of the term.

On the face of it, Being Slacker Better looks to be the ultimate foray into individualism.

I even saw it spelled out in an appraisal of mine once. In blue biro were the words, "Steve doesn't care about us, he just cares about himself".

IWhen I read this it just about killed me. It was so far from what I actually believed that for a minute I wondered if I'd read it wrong and they were talking about a different person. The fact that the writer had used my name was a give-away!

Me being me, I disregarded all the other positive comments from other people, because I simply couldn't shake this particular message; for days.

Collective well-being is where Being Slacker Better becomes sustainable

What made it harder was that the appraisal was anonymous. I had no idea who on my staff felt this way. Whoever it was, I was sure that they would have talked to others in my team about this. And if there's a brave soul prepared to write it (albeit anonymously) then there would no doubt be others who also have wondered about it too.

Where in my leadership had I painted this picture? What picture had I painted?

I could see a few possibilities.

Being Slacker Better isn't just about putting yourself first. It's about allowing **everyone** to re-examine what they believe is true, when it comes to the way they do and go about their work.

Obviously I hadn't communicated this clearly enough.
Just as importantly, we hadn't done enough team building and collaboration to nail the point through to everyone.

It's important to build a culture that understands collectively that everyone's well-being is good for everyone

I was never a non-caring, always thinking about myself, sort of a leader. I was, however, self aware enough emotionally to know that when I'd had enough I was prepared to do something about it - even if it might not look good through the optics.

Simple things like leaving school early when I was mentally burnt out for the day is a great example. For many staff they wouldn't see me arrive at school - I was always one of the first to arrive - because they weren't there. This didn't stop them from being judgemental if they saw me driving off while they were still sitting in a meeting at the other end of the day.

Interestingly I'd always drive away feeling very guilty. I needn't have worried - people would always like to think whatever they like to think anyway.

All of this sounds a little like sour grapes - it's not meant to. There's no doubt heaps of things in my career as a leader that I didn't get right. Instead I'm trying to paint a picture as to why it's important to build a culture that understands collectively that **everyone's well-being** is good for **everyone.**

Was my well-being paramount to everyone else's because I was the leader? Hell no!

But obviously there was a lot more that I could've done to build my team and to build a more collaborative body.

Here I'd like to talk a little about collective well-being.
I'm old enough to remember a time when "well-being" wasn't even a thing. Back in those days you just did what you were told and you were expected to "harden up" in order to get on with it. And if that didn't suit you, then tough luck.

I remember a conversation with a senior member on my team. I wanted to not only start talking about well-being, but actually start doing something about it.

The conversation wasn't a particularly successful one. My team member outwardly queried whether this was a thing we should be wasting our time on, and that she was worried it would just give people an excuse to "opt out" of the important work that needed to be done.

She essentially was saying that if we were going to begin to tackle well-being, then we were opening ourselves to a lot of slackness; it would be an affront on professionalism!

Collective well-being isn't a static state of affairs. It's a continuous journey of improvement for everyone. It requires ongoing reflection, adaptation, and action to address any emerging needs and challenges. There's nothing slack about that.

Collective well-being recognises that the health and happiness of one person is contagious. We're all connected, and the actions and conditions that benefit one person often benefit the wider team. There's nothing slack about that either.

Finally, collective well-being necessitates ethical considerations in decision-making. Choices in your team should always prioritise the greater good while respecting individual rights and autonomy. This can be a difficult thing to manage. Members on your team will no doubt be interested in the equality and equity of the decisions that you make in regards to individuals. Are you fair, and are you consistent?

This is where collaboration and team building comes in.
Building a sense of team is crucial to encouraging a well-being culture that is positive and sustainable. It involves many moving parts and needs to be nimble enough to help everyone through virtually any situation.

There are heaps of fun and interesting team building ways available on google. Take a look for yourself.

You're looking for things that will focus your team on improving relationships, fostering a positive team culture, and addressing any challenges or conflicts that may hinder team performance. The aim is to strengthen interpersonal connections, increase morale, boost motivation, improve team effectiveness and ultimately promote collective well-being.

Here are some of my favourite ideas:

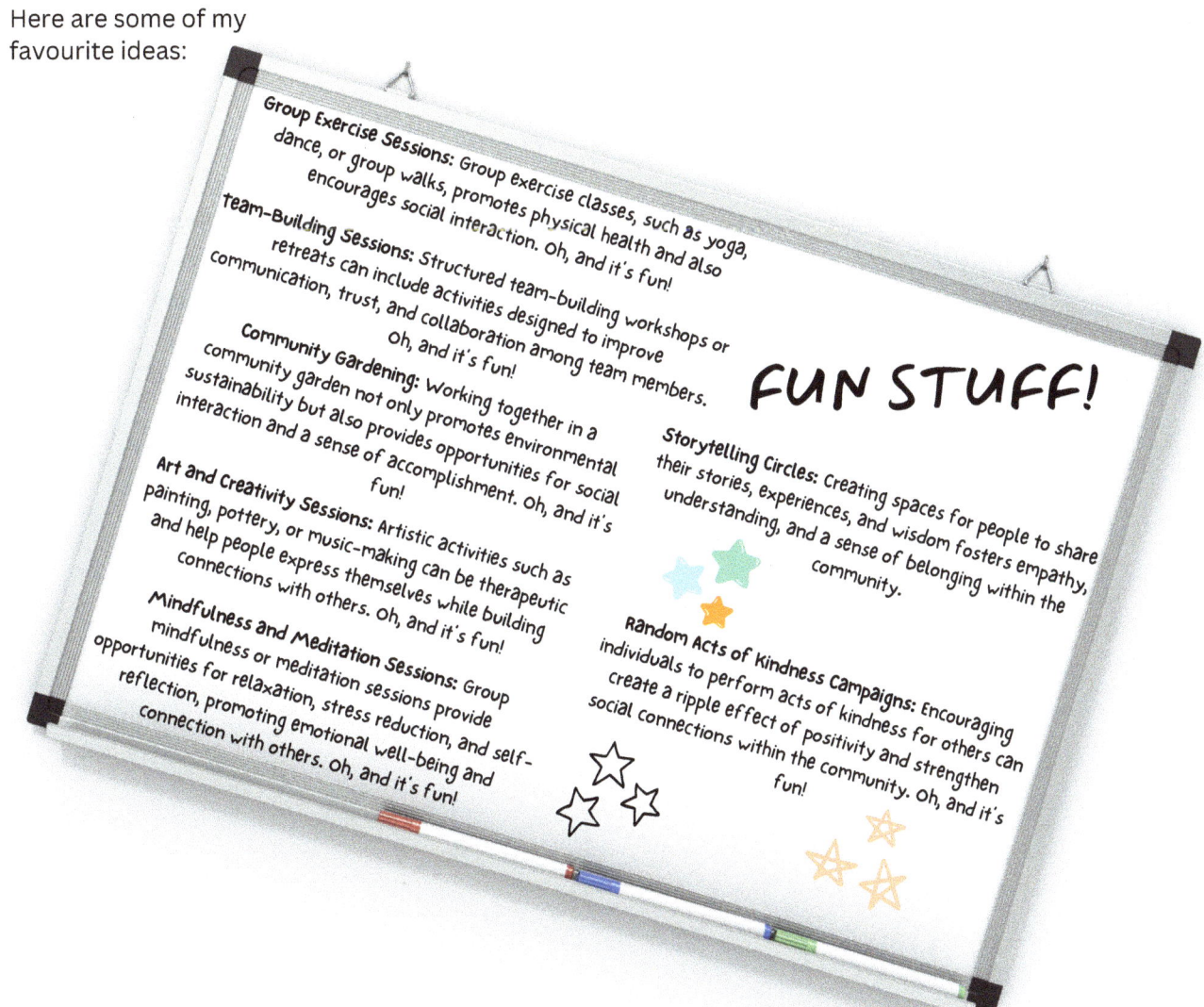

FUN STUFF!

Group Exercise Sessions: Group exercise classes, such as yoga, dance, or group walks, promotes physical health and also encourages social interaction. Oh, and it's fun!

Team-Building Sessions: Structured team-building workshops or retreats can include activities designed to improve communication, trust, and collaboration among team members. Oh, and it's fun!

Community Gardening: Working together in a community garden not only promotes environmental sustainability but also provides opportunities for social interaction and a sense of accomplishment. Oh, and it's fun!

Art and Creativity Sessions: Artistic activities such as painting, pottery, or music-making can be therapeutic and help people express themselves while building connections with others. Oh, and it's fun!

Mindfulness and Meditation Sessions: Group mindfulness or meditation sessions provide opportunities for relaxation, stress reduction, and self-reflection, promoting emotional well-being and connection with others. Oh, and it's fun!

Storytelling Circles: Creating spaces for people to share their stories, experiences, and wisdom fosters empathy, understanding, and a sense of belonging within the community.

Random Acts of Kindness Campaigns: Encouraging individuals to perform acts of kindness for others can create a ripple effect of positivity and strengthen social connections within the community. Oh, and it's fun!

You might be worried that these will take you away from the core business of your organisation. I mean, there's only so many hours in a day right?

Potentially this is true. The best way to get around this is by doing them in little bite sized sessions. Make them a natural part of your routine. They don't have to take over - just a little bit and often, and it helps build a culture of fun and even mischief!

Once again, as a leader, you need to get in and lead by example. Get involved in the fun times, show your lighter side, and, most importantly, show that you are open to promoting well-being in your workplace;

Be Slacker Together.

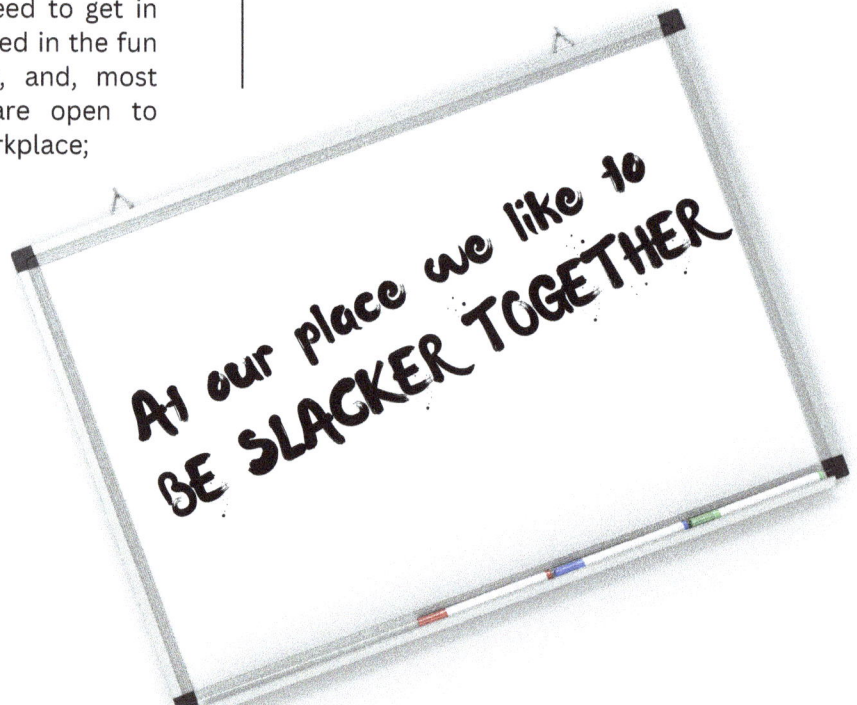

Cut yourself some slack – you're doing better than you think
– **Anonymous**

CHAPTER SEVEN
BE A SLACK PROFESSIONAL
PROFESSIONALISM AND THE CULT OF BUSYNESS

Recently I found myself in front of a crowd of motivated looking educationalists.

It was the end of the Summer holiday break and they'd all sacrificed the last few days of freedom to come along and listen to me and some other amazingly qualified educational innovators.

I felt in exalted company. Not only was I sharing the gig with three other presenters who were incredibly well respected in their fields and who "knew their stuff with a guru-like intensity. I was also standing in front of a whole heap of amazing New Zealand teachers and principals who day in and day out fronted up to the children in their schools with guru-like intensity!

What would I have to say and share that could come anywhere near being worth the sacrifice of giving up the last vestiges of their summer holiday?

I was there to talk about Being Slacker Better.

In reality I was there to talk about the school year that was about to start. The Be Slacker Better title, as I'm pretty sure you've cottoned on too, is just a nice little catch phrase to get everyone's attention.

At the beginning of the school year everyone is feeling refreshed. There's a sense of possibility and hope that permeates the air. And there's also new stationery. Pencils sharp and smart - nothing bitten, sucked, or jammed down the back of the couch. Felt Pens that actually write long beautiful lines, with colours that explode off the page, nibs exactly where they're meant to be and not force fed into the rear of the pen in a Herculean like manner. And there's paper too, reams and reams of it, waiting to have things expressed all over it without a dirty finger smudge, a scribble or dog ear in sight.

It's a beautiful time. And it lasts until it's not.

Has any one run a half marathon before?

I'm painting a picture for the teachers in the audience. I begin by asking if any of them have completed a half marathon run. A smattering of hands go up. Some have even run a full marathon.

I tell them that I've run seven half marathons. I can see they're feeling a little uneasy. What's running long, long distances got to do with school. Was I about to make them take a run around the block?

Then I tell them. They might not have run the distance before, but all of them had experienced it, because that's exactly what being in a school for a ten week term is like.

The days before school starts are a bit like the beginning of a half marathon.

Here the runners mingle around and everyone looks great. Many are wearing new active wear, or are sporting new shoes. Some are fidgeting with the music playlist on their devices. All are friendly and encouraging, smiling and hopeful.

It's the same in a school. Everyone is at the start line and everyone is looking really fresh. Some have bought new clothes, some are sporting new haircuts, and everyone has new stationery! All are friendly and encouraging, smiling and hopeful.

A school term is typically broken up into ten weeks. The half marathon is 21.25kms. Both are very similar in the way that they play out.

The first 5kms of the run is very much like the first 2-3 weeks of the term. There's a lot of positive chatter, support and encouragement going on. People continue to be helpful. The stationery resources are holding up in the classroom, as is the active wear in the race.

From 5kms through to 10, things begin to change. The runner might feel a little twinge in their calf. Is it that pesky old injury flaring up? The runner begins to feel the first stages of flagging energy, but yet they feel positive.

For the teacher, they've hit weeks 3 and 4. The reality of the term has arrived. Old habits in the school begin to flare like an old injury.

There's still a feeling of relative positivism and a sense of determination. Energy levels are pretty high but they begin to dip.

From 10kms through to 15km reality is more than settling in. The runner passes the halfway mark, and knows that although the next half is exactly the same length as the first, it'll be a lot harder.

That twinge in the calf has gone away, and it's now replaced with a nagging pain in the lower back. It's hard to run like this. There are doubts flowing through the mind. How far can they go on like this? Will they make it to the end?

There are doubts flowing through the mind. How far can I go on like this?

For the teacher they've hit weeks 5-7. Energy levels are falling. For some they're in free fall. It's hard to keep in mind that the time between now and the end of the term is less than the time that they have already travelled.

When the runner hits 18-20kms it's known as hitting the wall. Around you the race is deathly quiet. Gone is the encouragement and the words of best wishes. The pains and the injuries are flaring and each running step takes energy needed to run an aircraft carrier.

In the classroom this is now weeks 8-9. Often the feeling that you get can begin earlier in the term. During Covid I'm sure that I once saw it beginning in week 4. It's hard to keep your head up during this time. It's hard to keep motivated. Around you everyone else appears to be in their own world. Energy has dipped so far that it's reminiscent of running on the orange fuel warning light in your car.

Strangely schools like to put on big ticket events during these weeks; like a school fair, or a musical production, or some major professional development event. I say strangely because these sorts of events require a huge amount of energy, patience, goodwill, organisation and all round determination to accomplish. Most of which are completely lacking in a school during weeks 8 and 9. The school has effectively hit the wall.

When you get to week ten it's the equivalent of the last couple of kilometres in the run. If you can't see the finish line, you can definitely sense it. Around you can feel that spirits are beginning to rise; the light you see before you is turning out to be the light at the end of the tunnel and not the light of an on-coming train.

I'm watching the teachers in front of me as I tell them this. The room is eerily quiet. There are some who are nodding. I'm getting a real sense that they can empathise with this analogy.

It's a constant battle to make all the "stuff" fit in

I wonder out loud how we, as in the schools that we work in, get ourselves into this.

At the beginning of each term, found in virtually every staffroom around the world, is a term planner whiteboard. Initially this whiteboard is empty, just rows and columns ten down and seven across. Numbers are put in; the dates of the term lay ahead for all to see. But essentially the whiteboard is empty of any intent.

And then it begins - the adding of events. Quickly the term planner explodes into life, full of meetings, events, disco, working bees and stuff; plenty of "stuff" - stuff that makes the school not only run, but gives a certain cultural validity to it. The busier the better, or so it seems.

Invariably the bigger stuff like school musicals, or school written reports are stuck at the back end of the term. Quite often in the "hit the wall" weeks of week seven through to nine.

It's a constant battle to make all the "stuff" fit.

It's the busyness of the term that brings a certain so-called "professionalism" to the proceedings. An empty term planner just looks plain slack. There's no one really to guard the empty spaces on the term planner quite the same as those who guard the forever important and necessary events that have already been placed there; once on the planner, they simply **have** to happen.

So where does this professionalism come from? What even is it?

I'm asking the group sitting in front of me what they think professionalism means. Everyone has a definition. Everyone has something to say. No one has the same definition.

I share the Cambridge Dictionary version that says, "having the qualities that you connect with trained and skilled people, such as effectiveness, skill, organisation, and seriousness of manner".

There's laughter in the room, especially at the "seriousness of manner" part. What does that even mean?

What's your personal definition of being professional?

It's here where the rubber hits the road in terms of Being Slacker Better. People see "being slacker" as being the opposite of being professional. Yet no one really knows what being professional is really about. Everyone has an opinion, but I'd argue that if there is no agreed-upon common understanding of what 'professional' really means, then surely there is plenty of room to incorporate a sense of Being Slacker Better into an agreed definition.

Who said that it's not professional having blank spaces on the term planner if they're there with the intent to look after the well-being of the team?

Who said not having a staff meeting every week is unprofessional?

Who said going home at 3:30pm if your brain is fried and you've simply done all you can on some mid-winter, week seven, Wednesday is unprofessional?

Who said postponing a meeting to the following term because your team needs a break is unprofessional?
Who said taking on some extra load if someone else is struggling is unprofessional?

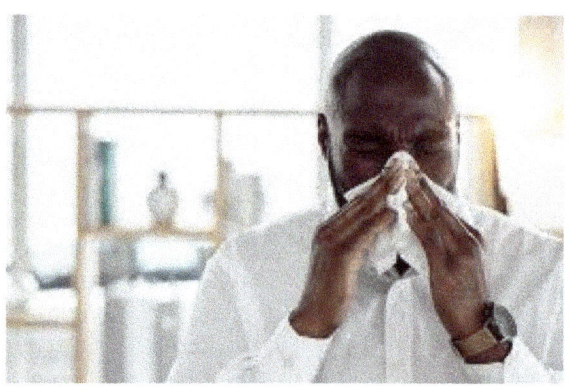

When I was young my mum would always make me go to school. The only thing that ever got in the way was if I had a temperature. If I had a fever then I was allowed to stay at home. Years later this seems to be a prevailing belief in a "professional" environment. Anything else is slack. Professionals shoulder on! Heavy colds?, anxiety?, stress?, nah! Take a concrete pill!

Instead we should be highlighting and being extra vigilant during those times in a school term, especially so in weeks seven through to nine. We should be the well-being police, looking after our people, protecting them and keeping them well. That's not slack, that's being professional.

Naysayers complain about those on their team who, once they take an inch, take a mile. They point to these people claiming that Being Slacker Better will make them even more slacker, and that now they'd have an excuse to be even more so.

I'd argue that these very same people have always found ways to "take a mile". Maybe they've actually had a masked "wellbeing" issue themselves, all along. Maybe Being Slacker Better will help their productivity - I'd be surprised if it didn't!

Who said going home at 3:30pm if your brain is fried is unprofessional?

The way you cope with people who like to manipulate situations negatively in a 'Be Slacker Better' environment is pretty much the same as you would in any situation: professionally.

- **Clarify Expectations:** You'd make sure that everyone on the team understands the purpose and boundaries of any well-being, or "allowing for slack" initiatives. You'd emphasise that you value employee well-being, and that work load issues are a collective well-being concern. And that you expect everyone to support everyone.

- **Open Communication:** You'd encourage open dialogue. Team members should be able to express concerns or suggestions regarding the well-being initiatives. This allows you to address any issues or misuse early on.

- **Together Set Limits:** You'd clearly define the parameters of the well-being initiatives. For example, you'd establish specific times or methods for taking breaks or participating in well-being activities.

- **Monitor and Evaluate:** You'd keep an eye on how the initiatives are being used and their impact on everyone in the team. If you notice misuse or abuse, you'd address it promptly and directly with the individuals involved.

- **Provide Support:** You'd offer support and resources to employees who genuinely need assistance with their well-being. This could include access to counselling services, flexible work arrangements, or training on time management and productivity.

- **Lead by Example:** You'd demonstrate a healthy work-life balance yourself and prioritise your own well-being. This sets a positive example for your team and reinforces the importance of balance in the workplace.

None of this sounds particularly unprofessional.

You can't use up creativity – the more you use the more you have – **Maya Angelou**

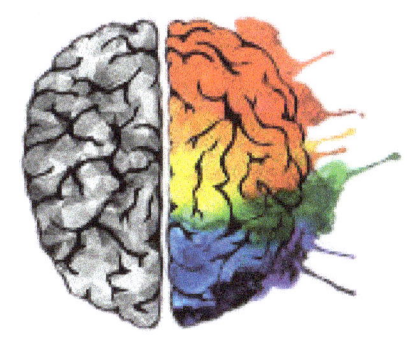

CHAPTER EIGHT
BE A CREATIVE SLACKER
INNOVATION AND CREATIVITY

The thing about Being Slacker Better is that it allows you to clear your diary for innovation and creativity, and I mean both individually and collectively.

It does this because you've cleared the air of all that stuff that used to leave all that foggy residue in your mind, all that stuff that you used to think was necessary. After all, it was the "professional way" of doing things. In reality, it was just getting in the way of doing the important stuff.

Here I'd like to remind you of what Viktor Frankl said even though I've already said it twice.

Remember how he said,

"Between stimulus and response, there is a space. In that space is our power to choose our response. In our response lies our growth and our freedom."
– **Viktor Frankl.**

Well, that "slack" amount of space that you have made yourself by Being Slacker Better gives you a massive amount of growth and freedom.

I'm getting excited just thinking of the things you could get up to in your schools or workplaces if you've managed to make that space. But truth be told I'd only be listing things from my own perspective. I have no idea what you could get up to!

Maybe, you don't either. Yet.

Maybe you'd feel an unnerving desire to fill that space with stuff that'll help you "get ahead". Maybe you'd write that report that you'd been putting off, or you'd finish that strategic plan that was never quite completed, or you'd empty the resource room of all the old slide projectors and OHPs from the 1970's.

That would be the natural instinct for dealing with that time that you had freed up, but it's not really the stuff that I'm talking about.

None of that helps you find meaning in your place. Yes it helps you with a purpose, and yes it'll tick a few boxes. But these are all ordinary everyday tasks. They're even tasks that maybe you could delegate to others.

Nope, I want you to think bigger than this.

To help you out I'd recommend taking a look at three ideas in order to get your innovative and creativity juices running.

1. **The VIA Strength Assessment.**

Remember in the second chapter when I talked about vision and meaning? I also talked about under-going the free online VIA Strength Assessment. As mentioned in that chapter this assessment is based on positive psychology principles and aims to help people discover and understand their core strengths in order to promote personal growth, well-being, and fulfilment. It'll list your core strengths and spits out a top 5 in super fast time.

By using your top five strengths in everything you do you're almost guaranteed to enhance your well-being, improve relationships around you, increase your resilience, perform better and be more authentic in how you deal with stuff.

If you're struggling to think of innovative ways to spend your time better, then finding tasks, and opportunities in your workplace that encourage the use of your own individual five strengths is a great place to start.

2. Five Ways To Well-Being

I've always been a big supporter of the Mental Health Foundation of New Zealand's "Five Ways To Well-Being". I like it because it is so simple, yet remarkably effective.

The Five Ways to Well-Being are:
Connect
Give
Take Notice
Keep Learning
Be Active

Not only are these great for your well-being but they are also wonderful starter points in finding things to do around your school other than completing that painful Strategic Plan or tidying out the Resource Room.

Try turning each of the five into questions e.g
What can I do to **CONNECT** with people? Or **HOW** can I **CONNECT** with others better?
What can I do to **GIVE** my time? Who can I **GIVE** my time too to help out?
How can I **TAKE NOTICE** of the little things going on around me better? What can I learn from **TAKING NOTICE** of these little things?
What sort of things can I do to **KEEP LEARNING?** What new skills or understandings do I need to make this school just a little bit better?
How can I use my time better to **BE ACTIVE?**

You can find more about the five ways to well-being at https://mentalhealth.org.nz/five-ways-to-wellbeing

3. **Te Whare Tapa Whā**

I love Te Whare Tapa Whā! It was developed by Sir Mason Durie in 1984 and represents the four dimensions of Māori well-being: physical, spiritual, family, and mental health. The model is represented by a wharenui, or meeting house, with four walls, each representing one of the four dimensions.

Like Five Ways to Well-Being it's predominantly a well-being model. Walk in to almost any school in New Zealand and you're likely to see the graphic of the Maori meeting house adorning the walls of the classroom.

As the New Zealand Mental Health Foundation tells us, "These walls represent taha wairua/spiritual wellbeing, taha hinengaro/mental and emotional wellbeing, taha tinana/physical wellbeing and taha whānau/family and social wellbeing. Our connection with the whenua/land forms the foundation.

When all these things are in balance, we thrive. When one or more of these is out of balance our wellbeing is impacted."

Using the names of the walls and foundations of the wharenui to help you generate new ideas to Be Slacker Better can be really useful.

You can find more about Te Whare Wha at https://mentalhealth.org.nz/te-whare-tapa-wha

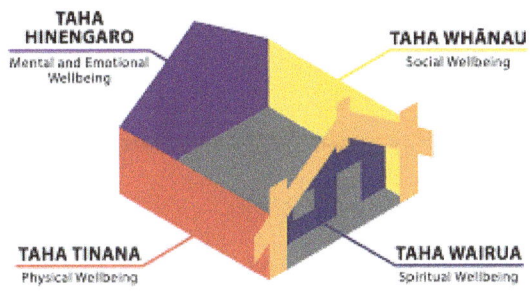

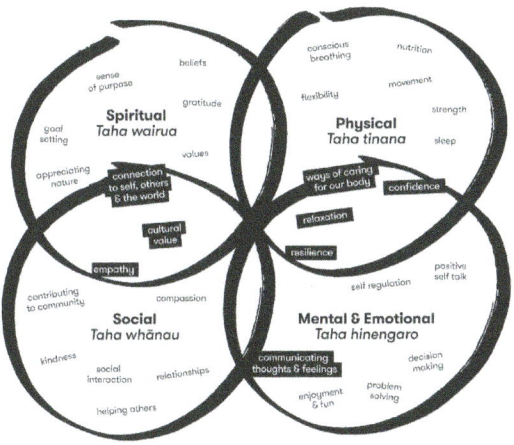

Acknowledgement Ella Sidey
https://www.ellasidey.com/blog/tewharetapawha

For example:

Whenua/land - Where are the physical places you feel nourished in? Or safe in? Is there somewhere other than your office, physically, that you could actually complete that pesky strategic plan from?

Taha Wairua/spiritual wellbeing - Is there somewhere that you can go that helps you feel better connected or grounded spiritually - whatever that may mean to you?

Taha Hinengaro/mental and emotional wellbeing - This is all about your heart, your mind, your conscience, your thoughts and feelings. Is there somewhere in your school where these sorts of things can be promoted for everyone? Is there a programme in the school that brings these needs to life in a natural, sustainable manner?

Taha Tinana/physical wellbeing - How can you refuel your body to make you mentally well? Remember, being mentally well is a crucial Leadership attribute. Sadly we often forget about it altogether, let alone talk about it. In the space you've made available by Being Slacker Better what can you do for your body? Are you taking care of yourself physically? Afterall physical health and mental health are always very much aligned.

Taha Whānau/family and social wellbeing - As a leader you have a unique role to play in your workplace. How do you nurture those family connections within your school? How do you make sure that your own family connections are also secure and that your professional life doesn't come before your family? How do you communicate this to your team?

You may have some other ideas, but I've certainly found these models to be a great place to start when I've looked to fill in the time and space made free from a Be Slacker Better attitude.

How can you refuel your body to make you mentally well?

Become the kind of leader that people would follow voluntarily, even if you had no title or position
– **Brian Tracy**

CHAPTER NINE
CONCLUSION
BE SLACKER BETTER

Being Slacker Better gives you permission to live your single-use life in a way, both professionally and personally, that honours the idea that you really only have one shot at this thing called life.

Where does this permission come from?

Well, it comes from you.

Unsurprisingly it always has.

Yes, there are times in our lives when we won't always have 100% control over what we do or how we respond. But for the most part, workplace included, we should always be in a position that we get to choose what we do, before we become unwell.

Does this mean not doing a lot of things? Not necessarily, but it does mean being self-aware of what we want out of our single-use life and preciously defending the right to live it in a manner that keeps us well. There is nothing slack about this

I never imagined that when I sent that text to my friend David, "Maybe we just need to learn to be slacker better", that this would eventually turn into a book.

The words that tumbled out of my fingers and into my phone that day, have now turned into a whole lot more words poured into this book. To me it all makes perfect sense. Hopefully it will to you as well.

Steve Zonnevylle

Do not love half lovers
Do not entertain half friends
Do not live half a life
and do not die a half death
If you choose silence, then be silent
When you speak, do so until you are finished
Do not silence yourself to say something
And do not speak to be silent
If you accept, then express it bluntly
Do not mask it
If you refuse then be clear about it
for an ambiguous refusal is but a weak acceptance
Do not accept half a solution
Do not believe half truths
Do not dream half a dream
Do not fantasise about half hopes
Half the way will get you nowhere
Half an idea will bear you no results
Half a life is a life you didn't live,
A word you have not said
A smile you postponed
A love you have not had
A friendship you did not know
The half is a mere moment of inability
but you are able for you are not half a being
You are a whole that exists to live a life
not half a life.
Khalil Gibran

ABOUT THE AUTHOR

STEVE ZONNEVYLLE

Steve is an articulate, creative, and passionate professional. He values the fostering of positive relationships and revels in working within team environments.

The majority of his working career has been in leadership positions in Education. He has nearly 30 years of Primary Principal experience in the New Zealand school setting. He brings to Thrive a multitude of skills that cross over successfully in many working environments.

His passions include music, writing and running.

THRIVE LEADERS

Our mission is to support and empower Leaders to thrive in their job - both professional and personally.

Join the Thrive Leaders Membership Today:

Here is what you will receive:
- Weekly newsletter with a topical focus
- Weekly article - exclusive to members, with practical ideas, inspiration and innovations
- Monthly Webinars on leadership, productivity, well-being and success strategies
- Monthly BookTalk interviews with authors on leadership, productivity and well-being
- Karpool Leadership: short inspirational chats with people in the know
- Full Access to the Thrive Leaders Library with replays, articles, bonus videos and extra content
- Discount codes for books, products and services (including our Wisdom & Wellness Retreat)
- and more...

Find out more at www.spectrumeducation.com or scan the QR code

www.ingramcontent.com/pod-product-compliance
Lightning Source LLC
Chambersburg PA
CBHW040752020526
44118CB00042B/2868